PIANO FUN
POP HITS
FOR ADULT BEGINNERS

Featuring Lead Sheets and Arrangements for the Beginning Pianist

Arranged by Brenda Dillon

CONTENTS

To access audio visit:
www.halleonard.com/mylibrary

3925-3043-3255-9074

ISBN 978-1-4584-2110-4

HAL•LEONARD®
CORPORATION
7777 W. BLUEMOUND RD. P.O. BOX 13819 MILWAUKEE, WI 53213

Visit Hal Leonard Online at
www.halleonard.com

PERFORMANCE NOTES

Introduction

Welcome to *Piano Fun: Pop Hits for Adult Beginners*, a collection of lead sheets and arrangements for the beginning pianist who has learned how to read music and wants to play easy arrangements of familiar melodies. The left hand accompanying styles include block chords, broken chords and notes that pass between the chords.

About the Orchestrations

There are two orchestrated accompaniment tracks for every song title. The first track is in a slower tempo for the lead sheet, and the second track is slightly faster for the song arrangement. The lead sheet track includes the melody and the arrangement track omits the melody, featuring only orchestrated harmonies.

To access the accompanying audio files, simply go to **www.halleonard.com/mylibrary** and enter the code found on page 1 of this book. This will grant you instant access to every file. You can download to your computer, tablet, or phone, or stream the audio live—and if your device has Flash, you can also use our **PLAYBACK+** multi-functional audio player to slow down or speed up the tempo, change keys, or set loop points. This feature is available exclusively from Hal Leonard and is included with the price of this book!

Fingering

Some finger numbers are circled in the music as a reminder to the player that one of these changes has occurred:

- The hand has moved to a different position.
- The RH thumb is passing under the 3rd finger.
- The LH thumb is passing under the 2nd or 3rd finger.
- A different finger number is used on the same note.
- The RH 2nd finger has crossed over the thumb.

Triads/Chords

- Triads are three note chords and seventh chords have four notes.
- Major triads built on the white piano keys can be divided into three sets:

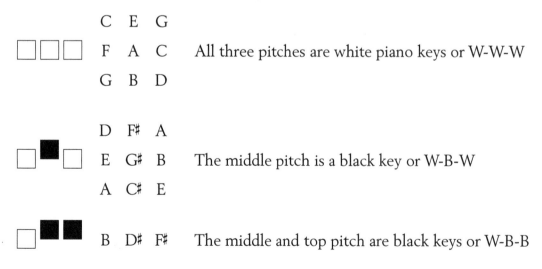

	C	E	G	
	F	A	C	All three pitches are white piano keys or W-W-W
	G	B	D	
	D	F♯	A	
	E	G♯	B	The middle pitch is a black key or W-B-W
	A	C♯	E	
	B	D♯	F♯	The middle and top pitch are black keys or W-B-B

- Minor triads have a small *m* by the alphabet letter (Cm). They are found by lowering the middle pitch of a major triad to the nearest piano key:

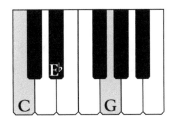

- Seventh chords are spelled with four notes. (G7 = GBDF). The bottom note is the root, the next note above is the 3rd, the note above the 3rd is the 5th, and the top note is the 7th. Some players choose to leave out the 5th of the chord, which is the next to top pitch.

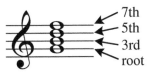

Root or Close Position

Chords can be played in two positions—root or close position. Learning to play close position chords is helpful because the hand doesn't have to skip around as much. Also, chords sound best when they are played in the octave below middle C, and close position chords make this easier.

- When the name of the chord is on the bottom, it's called root position. (CEG)
- When another pitch of the chord is on the bottom, it's called an inversion.
- Close position is found by moving to the nearest chord tones rather than having the hand move from root to root.

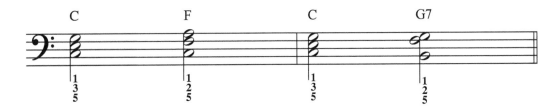

Accompanying Styles

Accompanying styles are usually played by the left hand. These arrangements use three accompaniment styles.

- Block chords (root or close position)

- Broken chords

- Passing tones move between chord tones.

All My Loving

Words and Music by John Lennon
and Paul McCartney

All My Loving

Words and Music by John Lennon
and Paul McCartney

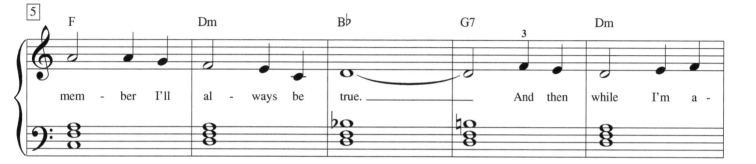

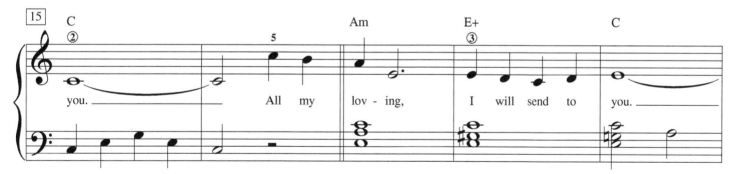

Are You Lonesome Tonight?

Words and Music by Roy Turk
and Lou Handman

Are You Lonesome Tonight?

Words and Music by Roy Turk
and Lou Handman

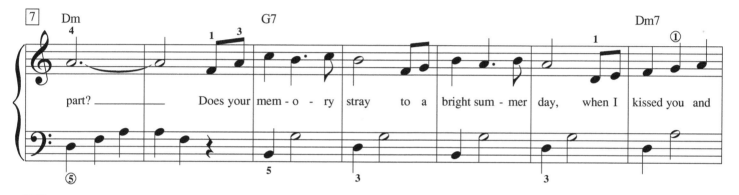

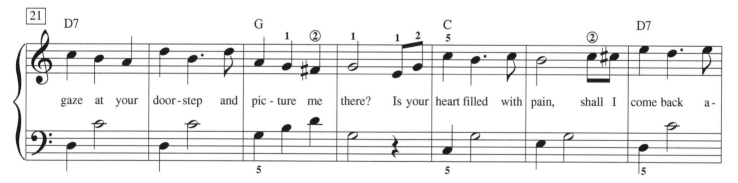

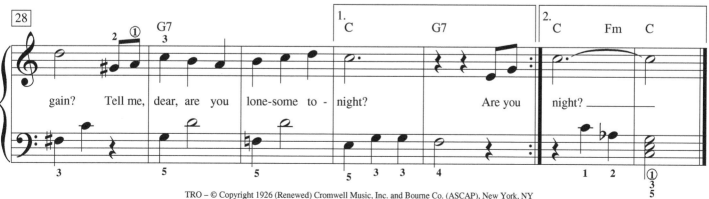

Forrest Gump – Main Title

(Feather Theme)
from the Paramount Motion Picture FORREST GUMP

Music by Alan Silvestri

Forrest Gump – Main Title

(Feather Theme)
from the Paramount Motion Picture FORREST GUMP

Music by Alan Silvestri

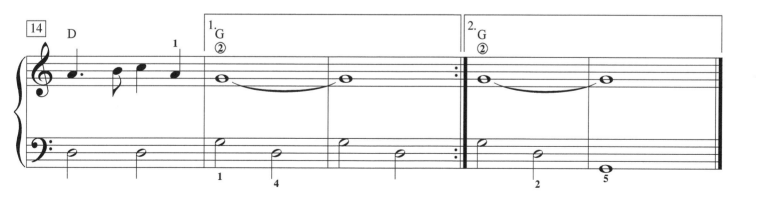

My Girl

Words and Music by William "Smokey" Robinson
and Ronald White

My Girl

Words and Music by William "Smokey" Robinson
and Ronald White

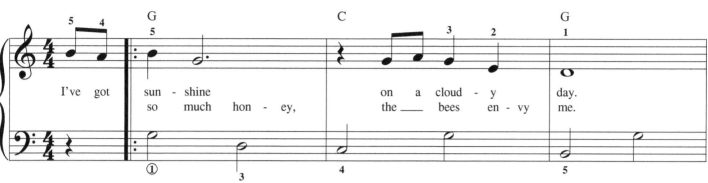

I've got | sun - shine | on a cloud - y | day.
so much hon - ey, | the ___ bees en - vy | me.

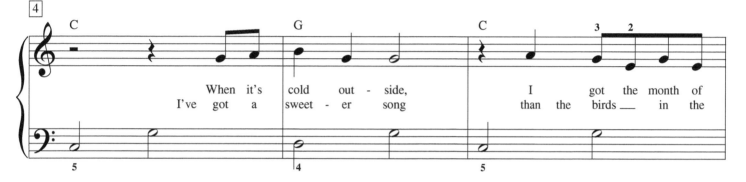

When it's | cold out - side, | I | got the month of
I've got a | sweet - er song | than the birds ___ in the

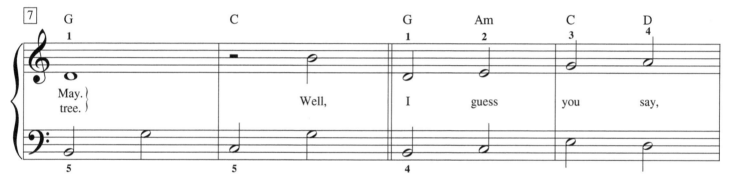

May. tree. | Well, | I | guess | you | say,

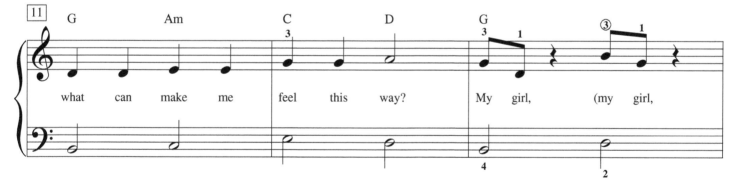

what can make me | feel this way? | My girl, | (my girl,

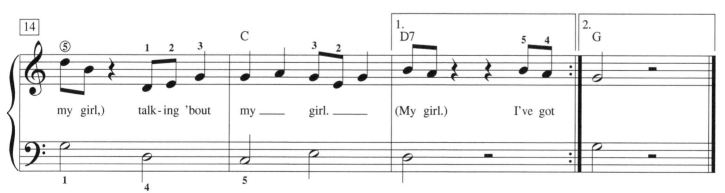

my girl,) | talk - ing 'bout | my ___ girl. | (My girl.) | I've got

The Sound of Silence

Words and Music by
Paul Simon

The Sound of Silence

Words and Music by
Paul Simon

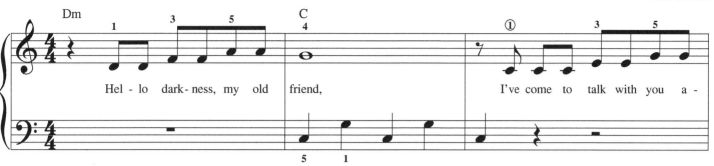

Hel - lo dark - ness, my old friend, I've come to talk with you a -

gain, be - cause a vi - sion soft - ly creep - ing

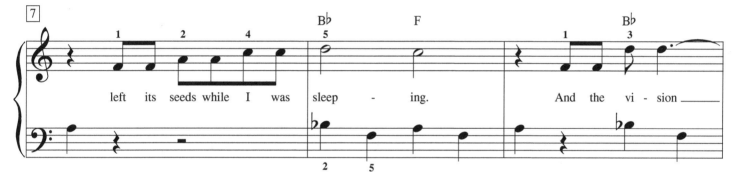

left its seeds while I was sleep - ing. And the vi - sion

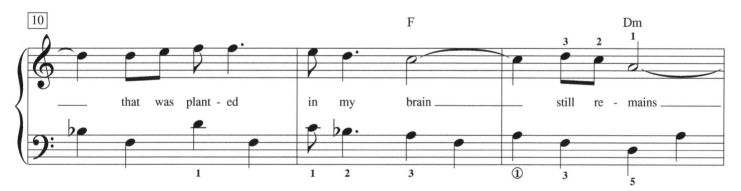

that was plant - ed in my brain still re - mains

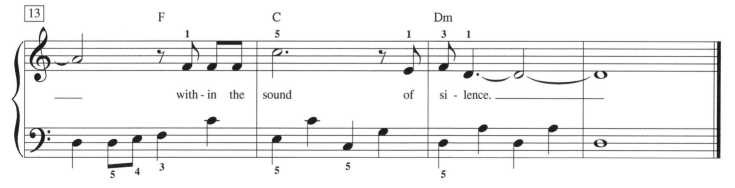

with - in the sound of si - lence.

Welcome to My World

Words and Music by Ray Winkler
and John Hathcock

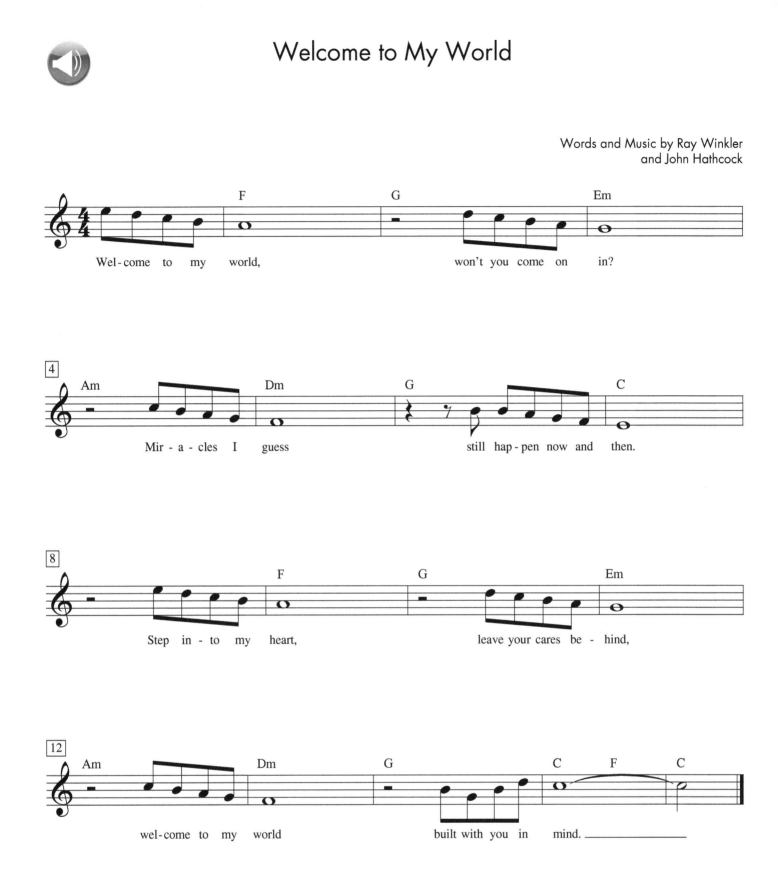

Welcome to My World

Words and Music by Ray Winkler
and John Hathcock

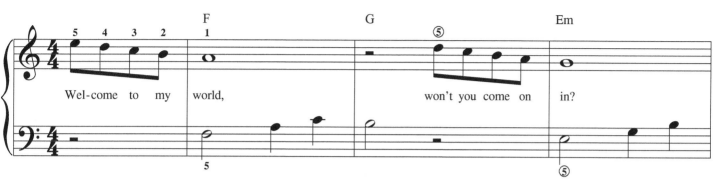

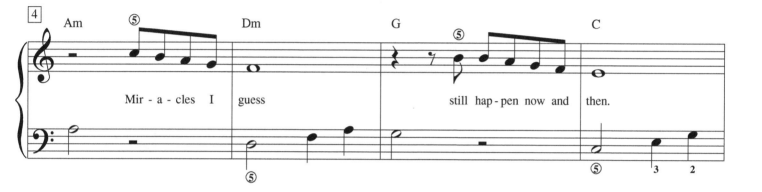

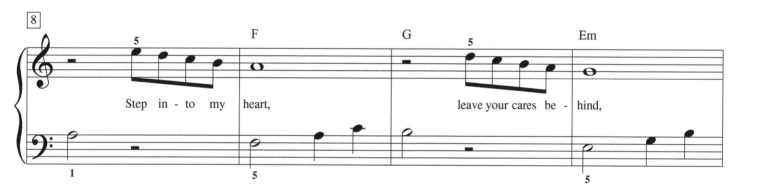

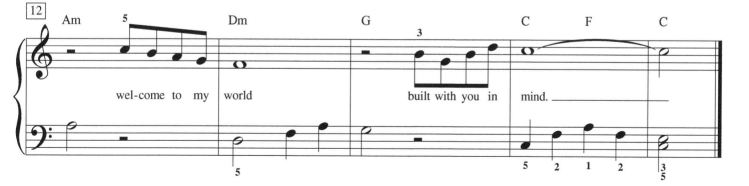

Imagine

Words and Music by
John Lennon

18

Imagine

Words and Music by
John Lennon

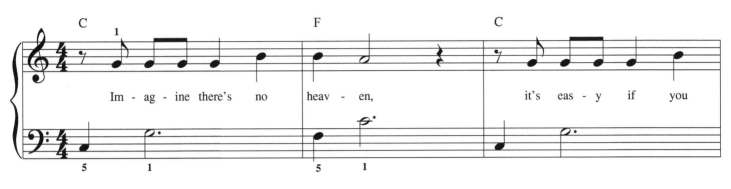

Im - ag - ine there's no heav - en, it's eas - y if you

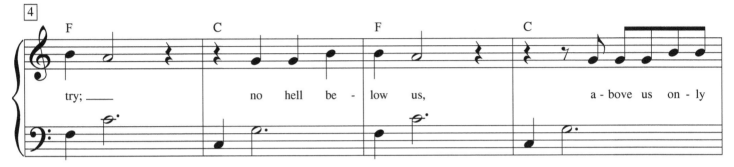

try; ____ no hell be - low us, a - bove us on - ly

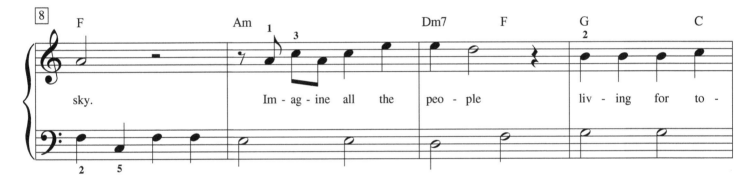

sky. Im - ag - ine all the peo - ple liv - ing for to -

day, ah. ____ Im - ag - ine there's no coun - tries,
Im - ag - ine no pos - ses - sions,

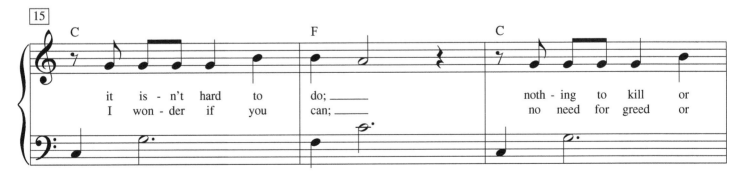

it is - n't hard to do; ____ noth - ing to kill or
I won - der if you can; ____ no need for greed or

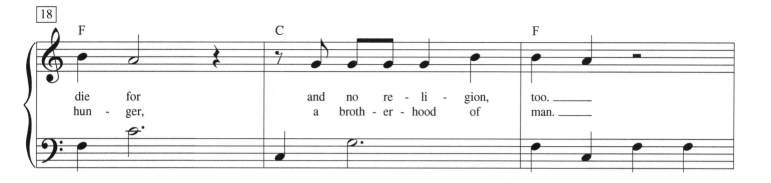

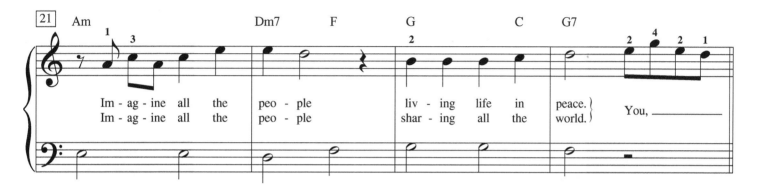

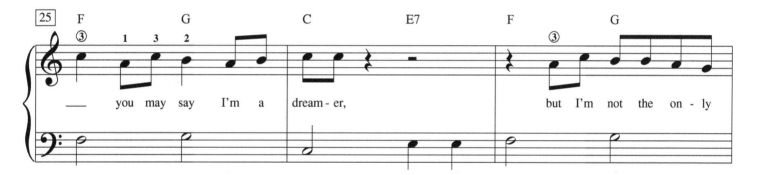

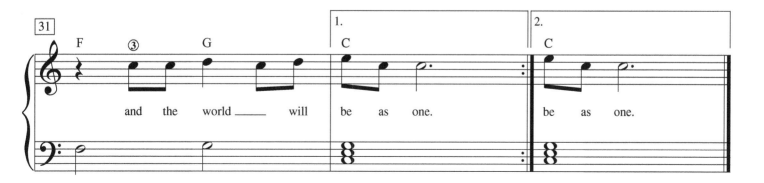

He's Got the Whole World in His Hands

Traditional Spiritual

Memory
from CATS

Music by Andrew Lloyd Webber
Text by Trevor Nunn after T.S. Eliot

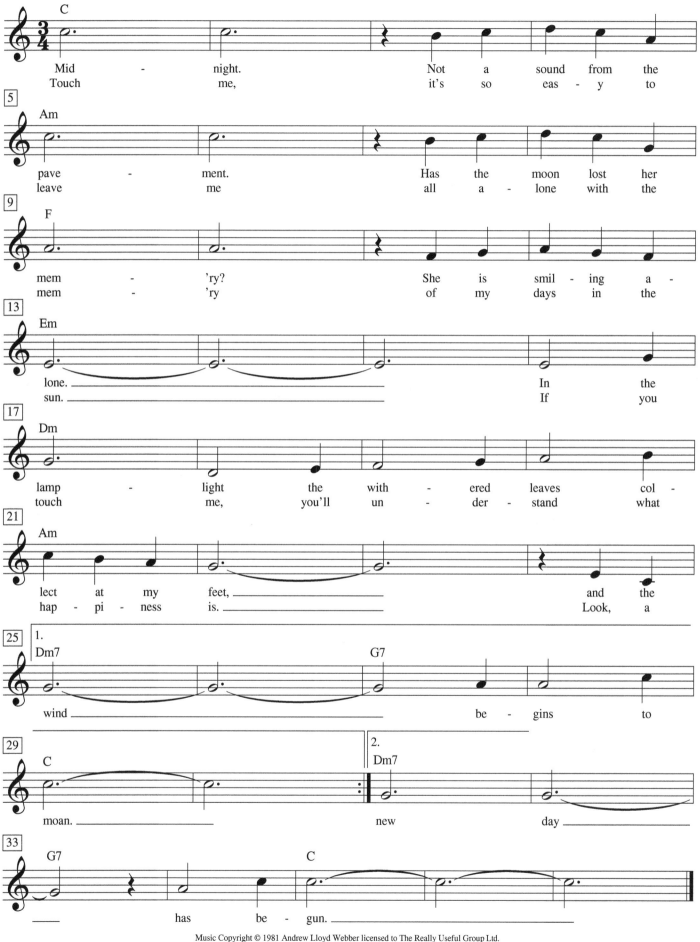

He's Got the Whole World in His Hands

Traditional Spiritual

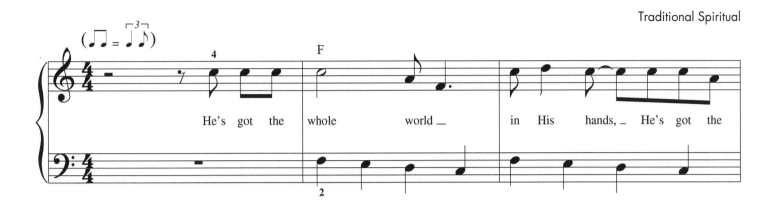

He's got the whole world __ in His hands, __ He's got the

whole world __ in His hands, __ He's got the whole world __

in His hands, __ He's got the whole world in His hands. He's got the

wind and the rain __ in His hands, __ He's got the wind and the rain __

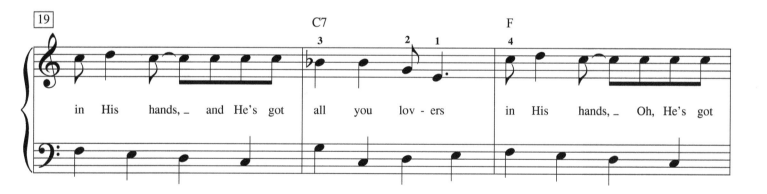

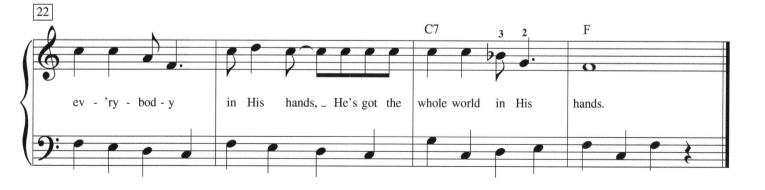

Memory
from CATS

Music by Andrew Lloyd Webber
Text by Trevor Nunn after T.S. Eliot

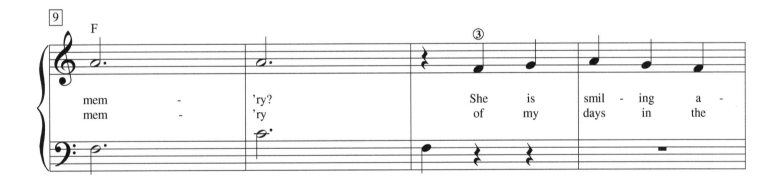

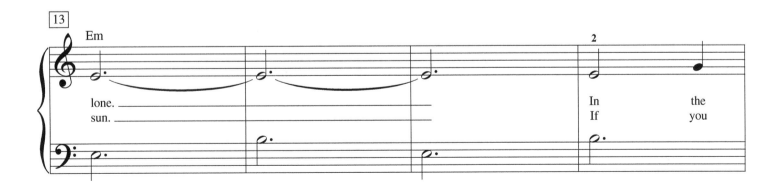

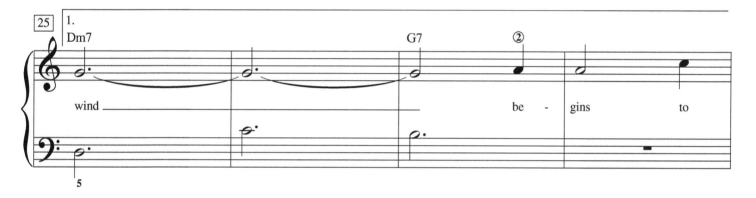

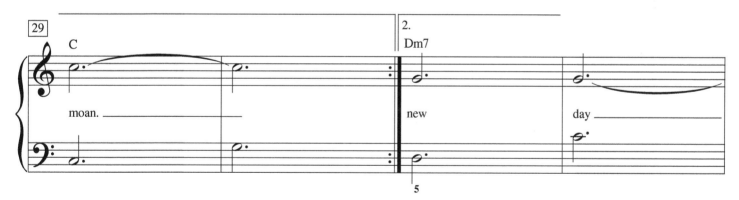

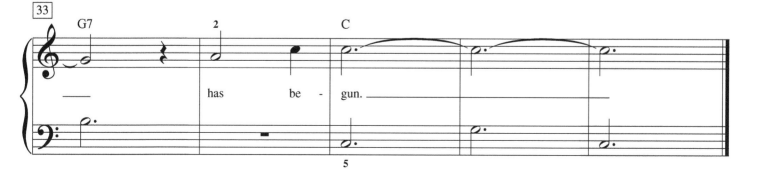

Moon River

from the Paramount Picture BREAKFAST AT TIFFANY'S

Words by Johnny Mercer
Music by Henry Mancini

Que Sera, Sera
(Whatever Will Be, Will Be)

Words and Music by Jay Livingston
and Ray Evans

Moon River

from the Paramount Picture BREAKFAST AT TIFFANY'S

Words by Johnny Mercer
Music by Henry Mancini

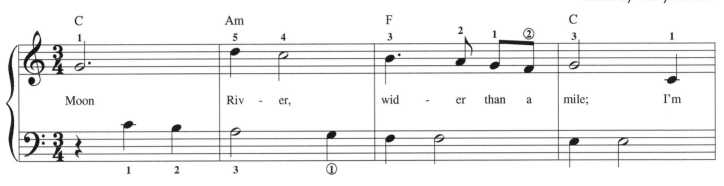

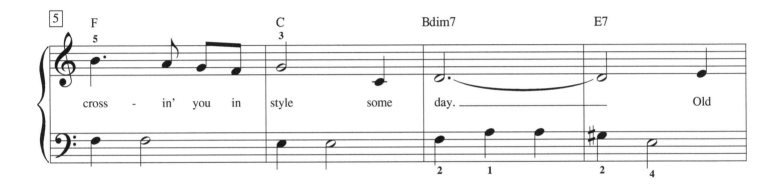

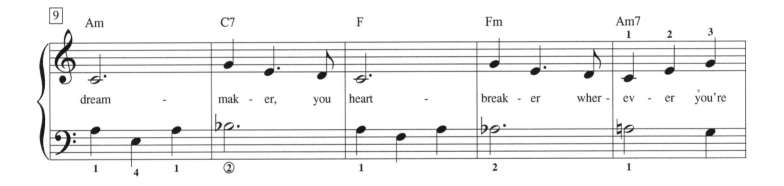

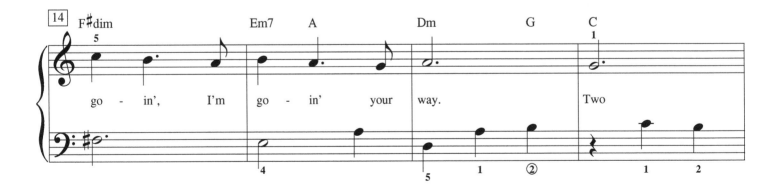

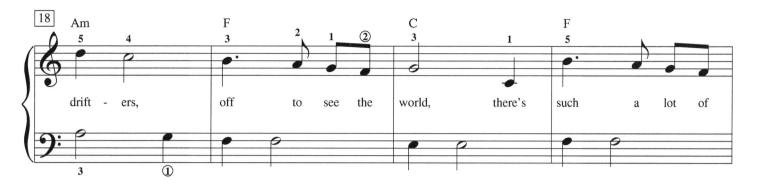

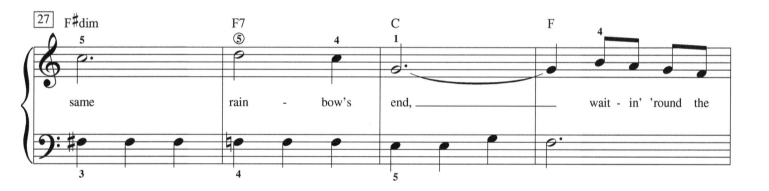

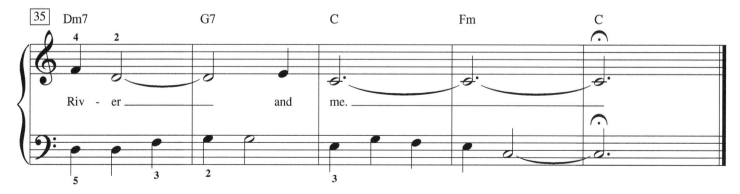

Que Sera, Sera
(Whatever Will Be, Will Be)

Words and Music by Jay Livingston
and Ray Evans

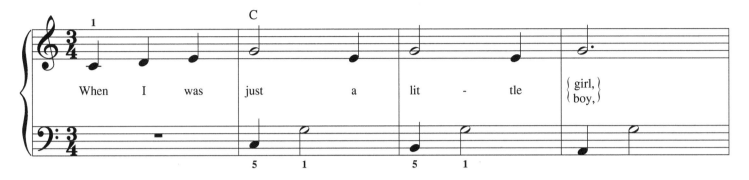

When I was just a lit - tle {girl,/boy,}

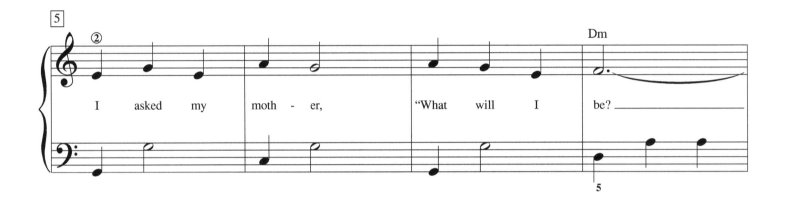

I asked my moth - er, "What will I be? ____

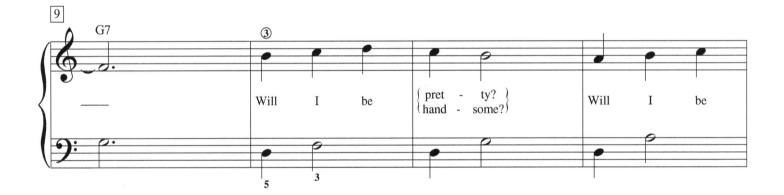

____ Will I be {pret - ty?/hand - some?} Will I be

rich?" Here's what she said to me:

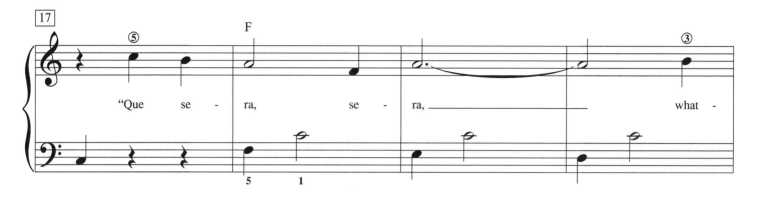

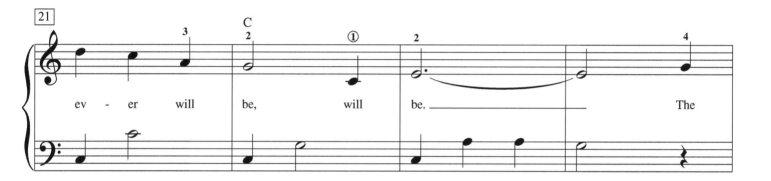

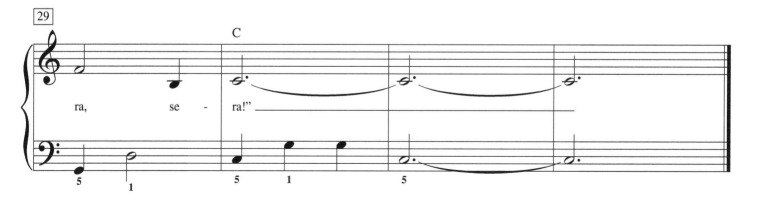

Stand By Me

Words and Music by Jerry Leiber,
Mike Stoller and Ben E. King

What a Wonderful World

Words and Music by George David Weiss
and Bob Thiele

Lyrics:

I see trees of green, red ros- es, too;
I see them bloom
skies of blue and clouds of white, the bright blessed day

for me and you,
the dark sacred night, and I think to my- self, "What a won- der- ful

1. world." I see
2. world." The

col- ors of the rain- bow, so pret- ty in the sky, are al- so on the fac- es of

peo- ple go- in' by. I see friends shak- in' hands, say- in', "How do you do?"

They're real- ly say- in', "I love you." I hear ba- bies cry, I

watch them grow; they'll learn much more than I'll ev- er know, and I

think to my- self, "What a won- der- ful world." Yes, I

think to my- self, "What a won- der- ful world."

Stand By Me

Words and Music by Jerry Leiber,
Mike Stoller and Ben E. King

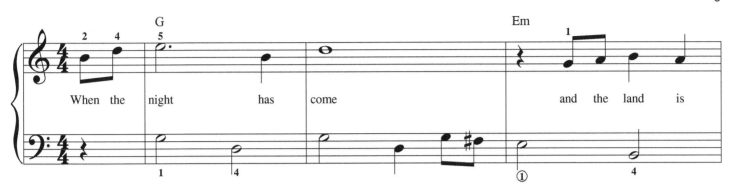

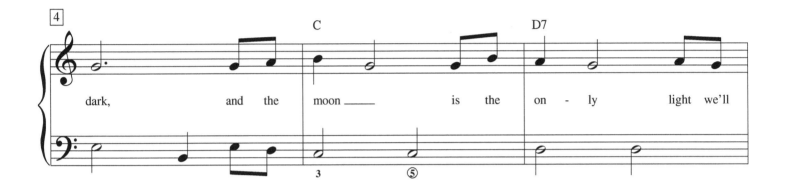

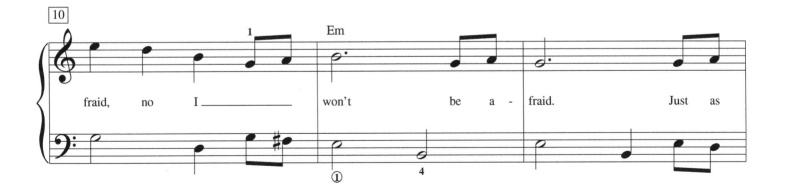

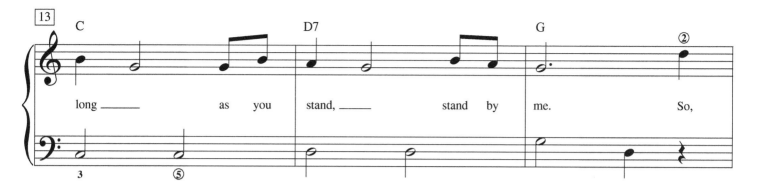

long _____ as you stand, _____ stand by me. So,

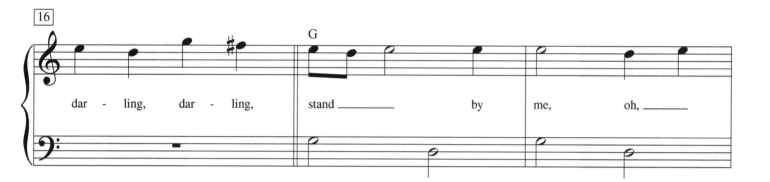

dar - ling, dar - ling, stand _____ by me, oh, _____

stand by me. Oh, stand, _____

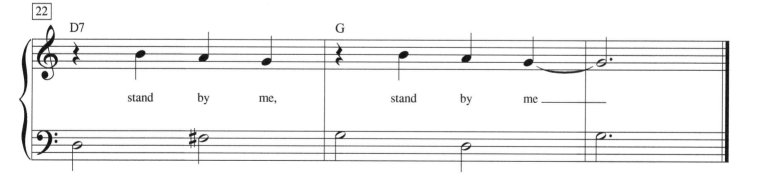

stand by me, stand by me _____

What a Wonderful World

Words and Music by George David Weiss
and Bob Thiele

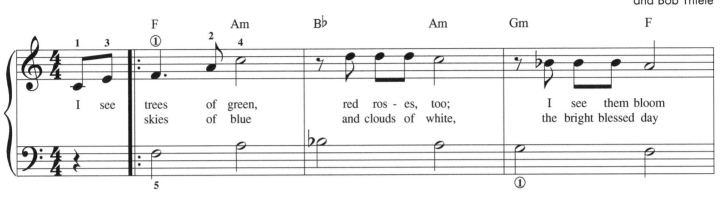

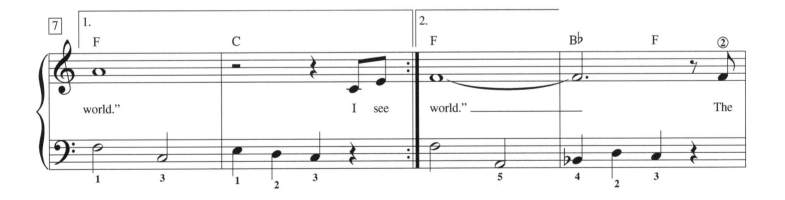

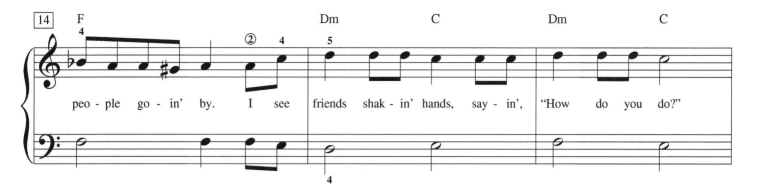

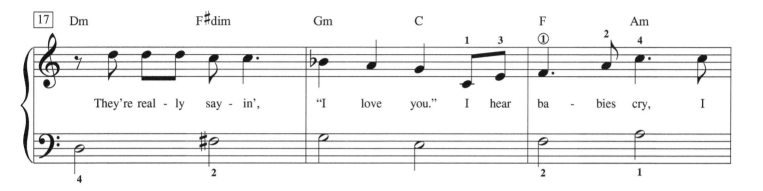

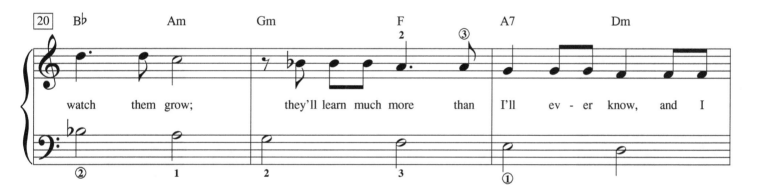

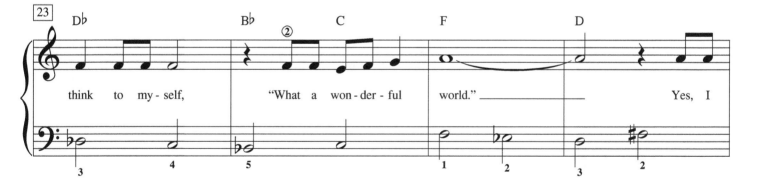

KEYBOARD CHARTS

Chords built on white piano keys:

C Major Chord

C E G

C7 Chord

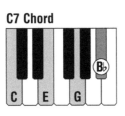

C E G B♭

D Major Chord

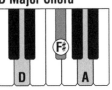

D A

D7 Chord

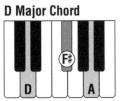

D A C

Dm Chord

D F A

Dm7 Chord

D F A C

Em Chord

E G B

E7 Chord

E G♯ B D

E+ Chord

E G♯ B♯

F Major Chord

F A C

F7 Chord

F A C E♭

Fm Chord

F A♭ C

G Major Chord

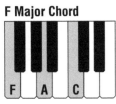

G B D

G7 Chord

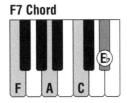

G B D F

Gm Chord

G B♭ D

Gm7 Chord

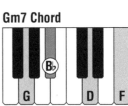

G B♭ D F

A Major Chord

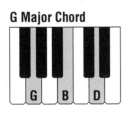

A C♯ E

A7 Chord

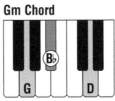

A C♯ E G

Am Chord

A C E

Am7 Chord

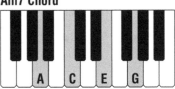

A C E G

Bdim7 Chord

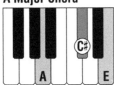

B D F A

Chords built on black piano keys:

B♭ Major Chord

B♭ D F

D♭ Major Chord

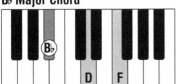

D♭ A♭ F

F♯dim Chord

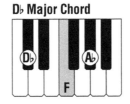

F♯ A C

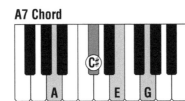
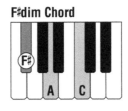